Copyright © 2018 San V. Paulin

All rights reserved. No part of this publication may be reproduced, distributed, or transmitted in any form or by any means, including photocopying, recording, or other electronic methods, without the prior written permission of the publisher, except in the case of brief quotations embodied in critical reviews and certain other noncommercial uses permitted by copyright law.

ISBN: 978-1-945532-93-1

Library of Congress Number: 2018911904

Published by:
Opportune Independent Publishing Company

Written by:
San V. Paulin

Illustrated by:
Rain W. Patton

Printed in the United States of America

For permission requests, write to the publisher, addressed "Attention: Permissions Coordinator," at the address below.

info@opportunepublishing.com
www.opportunepublishing.com

It was a beautiful Saturday morning and little Kian woke up with a BIG yawn *"OOooouuaah"* and a l o n g stretch of his little boy arms.

He made his hands into fists and rubbed his little boy eyes.

He jumped out of bed excitedly, *"Daddy, Daddy, what are we doing today?"*

"Good morning buddy," said Daddy.

"Good morning Daddy," said Kian as he flung his arms around Daddy's neck

and gave him a BIG hug.

"Daddy, it's Saturday, what are we doing today?" Kian eagerly asked.

"Well, would you like to go feed the ducks with me?" asked Daddy.

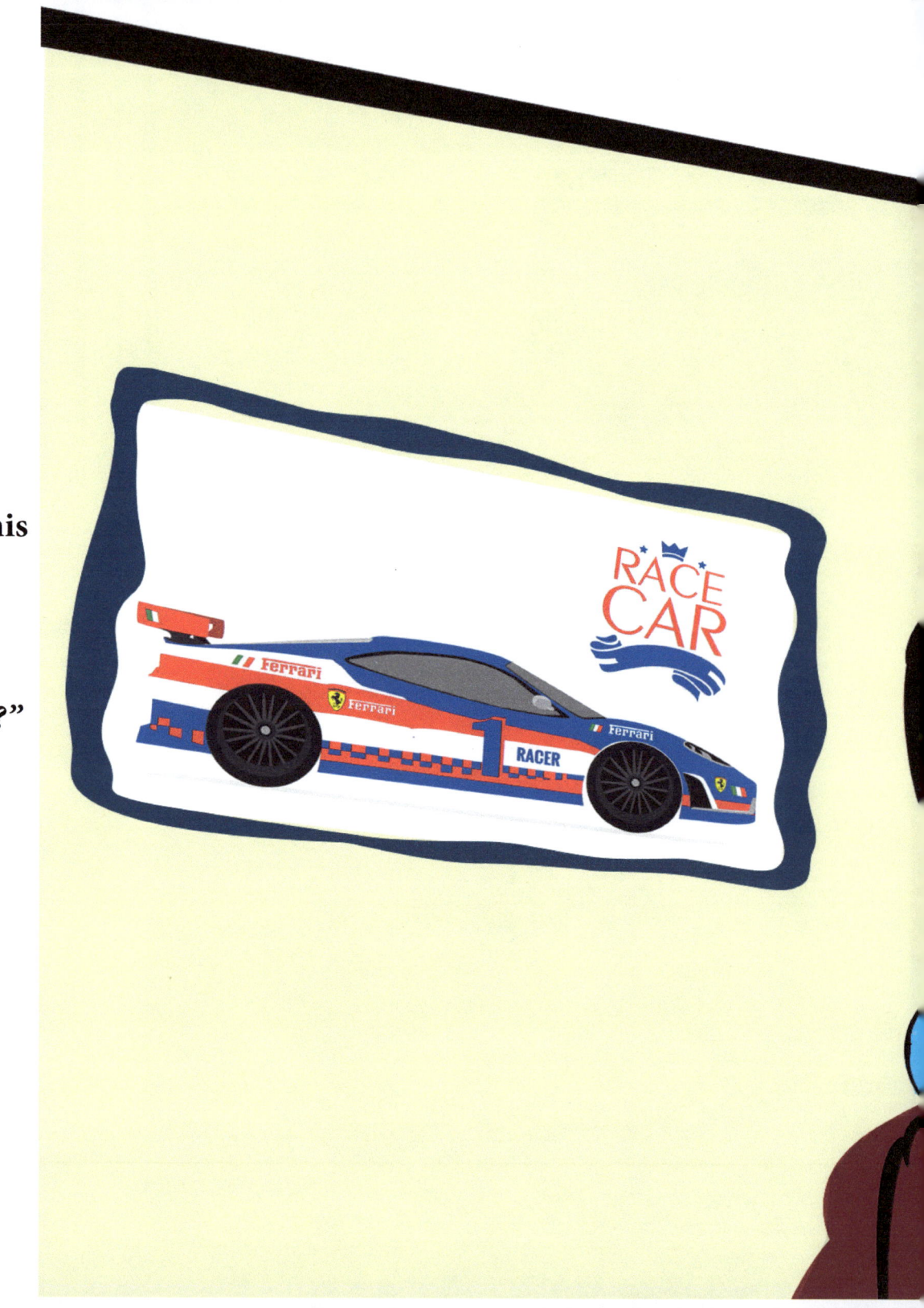

"Yes, yes, yes!

I want to feed the ducks!" Kian said jumping up and down with arms in the air with excitement.

Kian hurried and ate his breakfast and then Daddy helped him to brush his teeth and change out of his pajamas.

"Now, are we ready to go feed the ducks, Daddy?" asked Kian. *"All ready!"* answered Daddy.

Daddy and Kian walked to the neighborhood park, and what did he see?

He saw lots of ducks and little ducklings.

He was so excited and wanted to feed them right away.

Daddy gave Kian a handful of cracked corn. *"Now Kian, be careful and do not get too close, we don't want to scare the ducks away." "Okay, Daddy!"* said Kian.

Kian walked *s l o w l y* towards a mother duck with his hand out full of cracked corn.

The mother duck suddenly went, *"quack, quack, quack"* as she approached Kian's hand. Kian surprised by the duck, took off running, *"aaaahhh, aaaahhhh, aaaahhh"* away from the mother duck.

He ran and ran as fast as he could. *"Kian, Kian, it's okay buddy,"* called Daddy as he ran and caught up to him.

"It's okay buddy, I won't let the ducks hurt you," Daddy gave Kian a hug and made him feel better.

"Now, let's try feeding the ducks again," said Daddy. *"Okay, Daddy!"* agreed Kian.

Daddy gave Kian another handful of cracked corn. *"Now buddy, throw the corn on the ground in front of the ducks."*

Kian did as his daddy said.

They watched the ducks peck the cracked corn as they talked.

Daddy and Kian walked home and Kian told his mommy all about his adventure of feeding ducks with Dadday.

The End.

www.ingramcontent.com/pod-product-compliance
Lightning Source LLC
Chambersburg PA
CBHW042108090526

44591CB00004B/46